Nirvana Printing Press

100 incredibili mandala per cambiare la tua vita

Libro da colorare

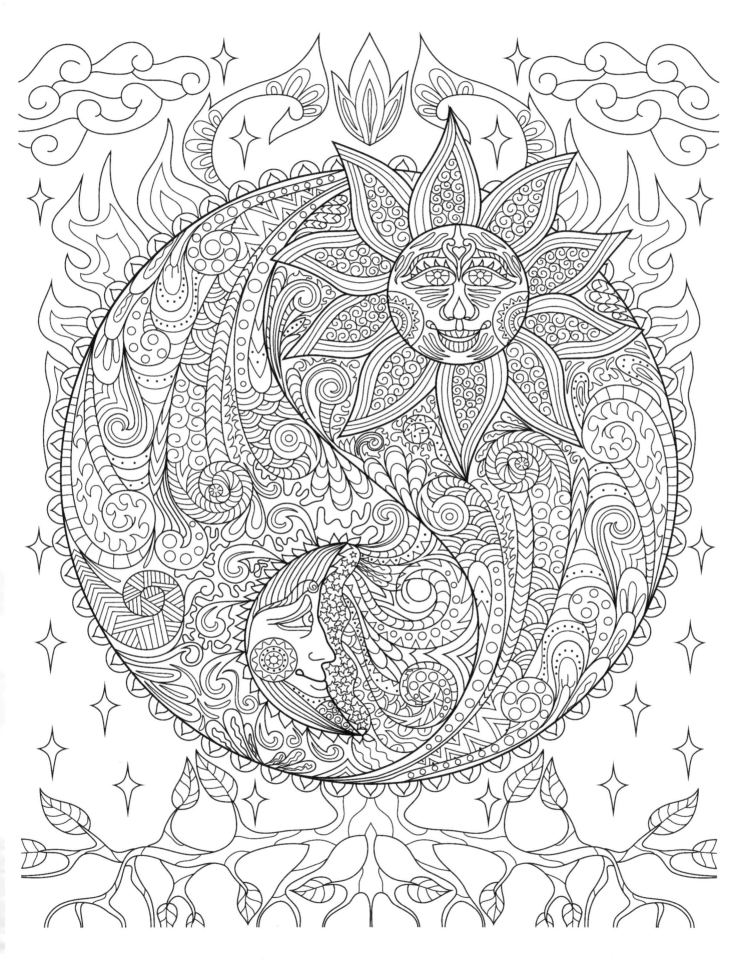

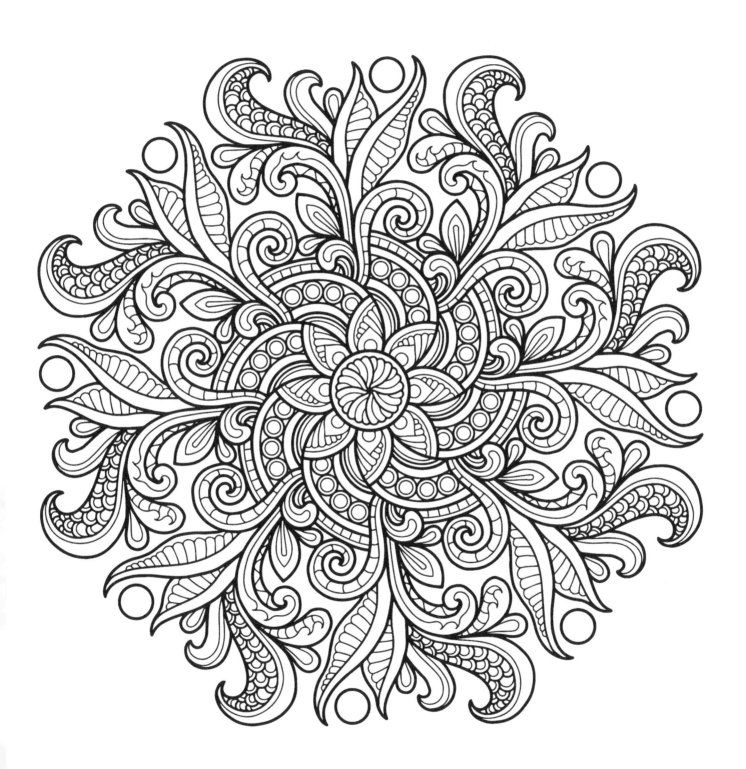

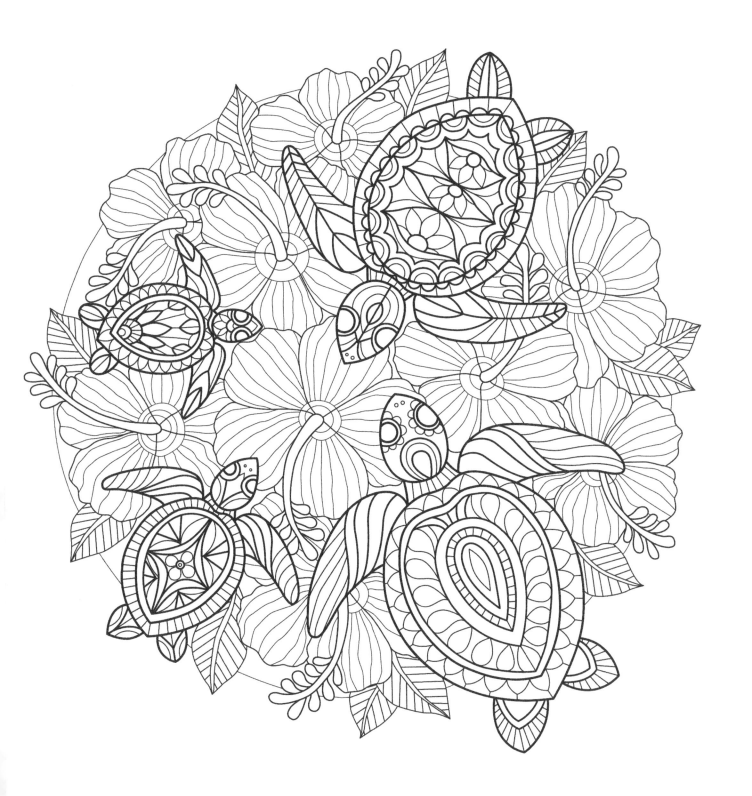

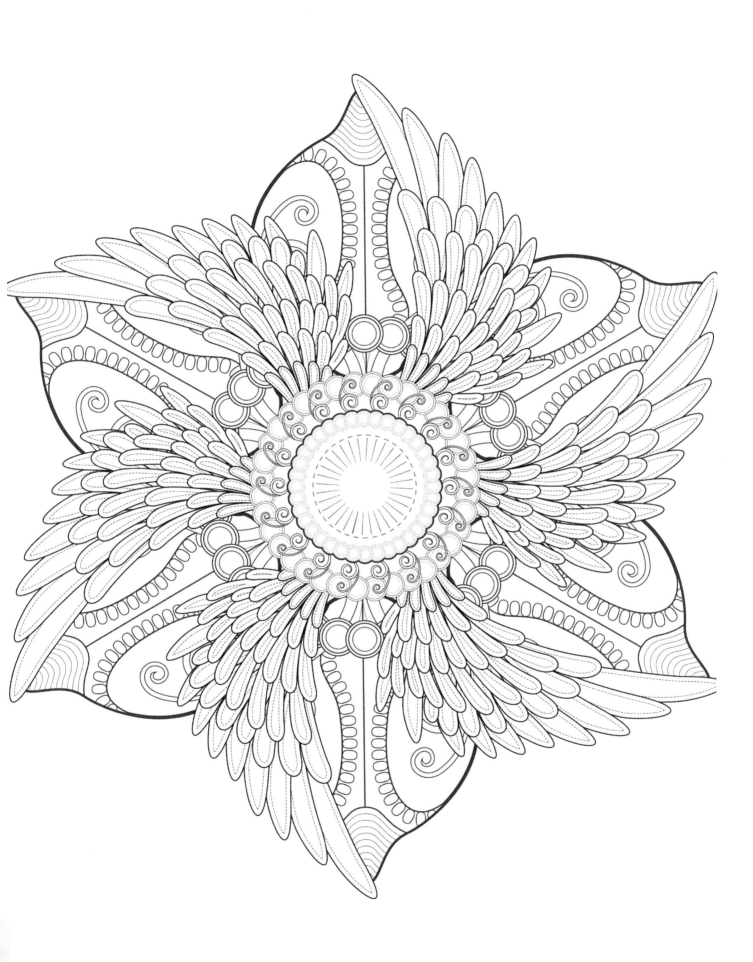

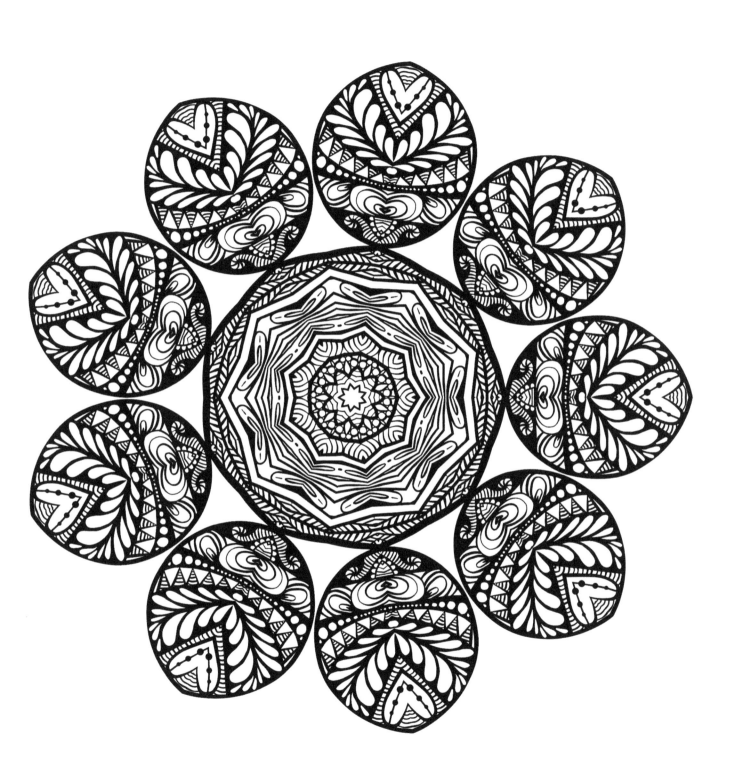

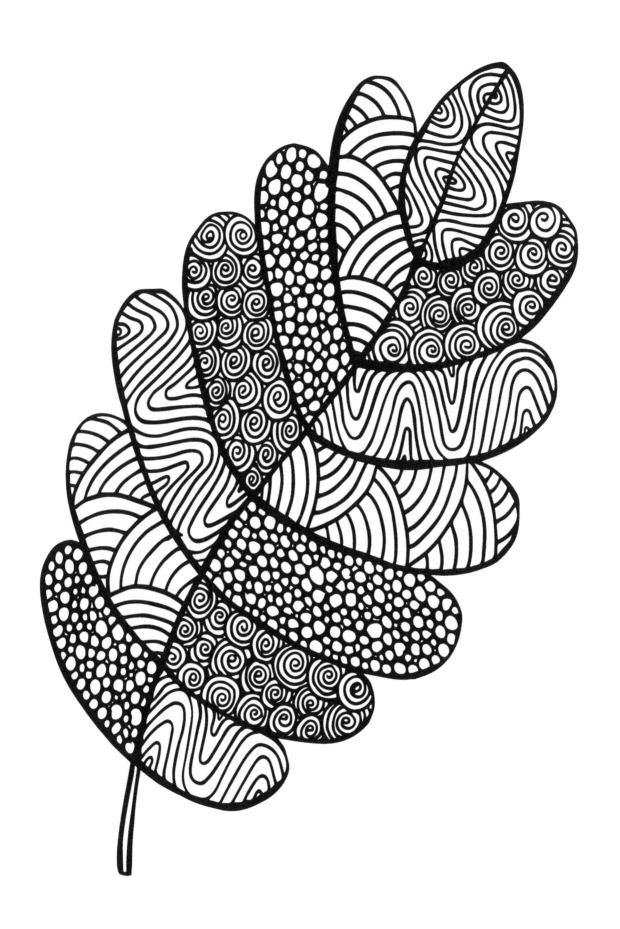

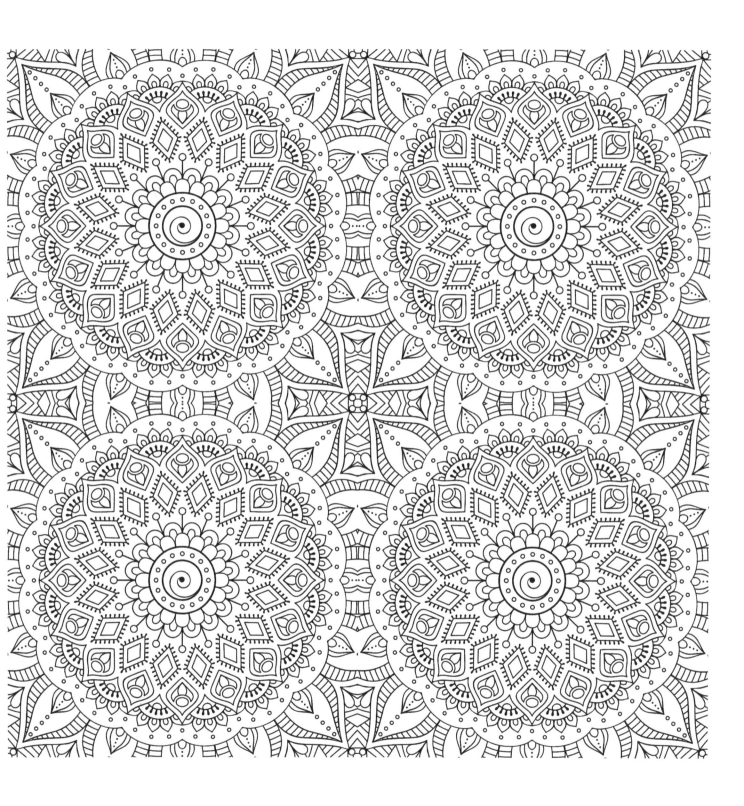

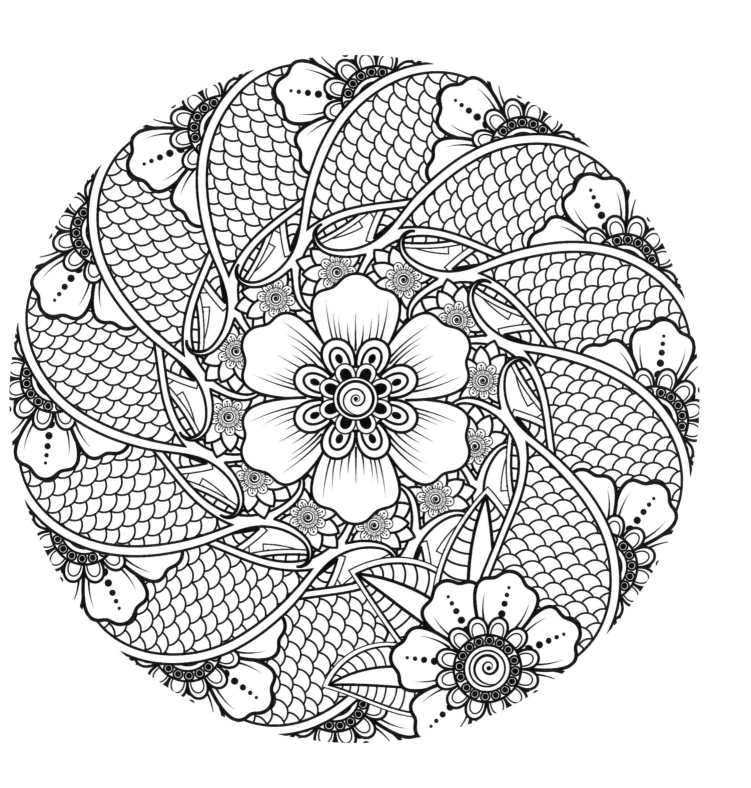

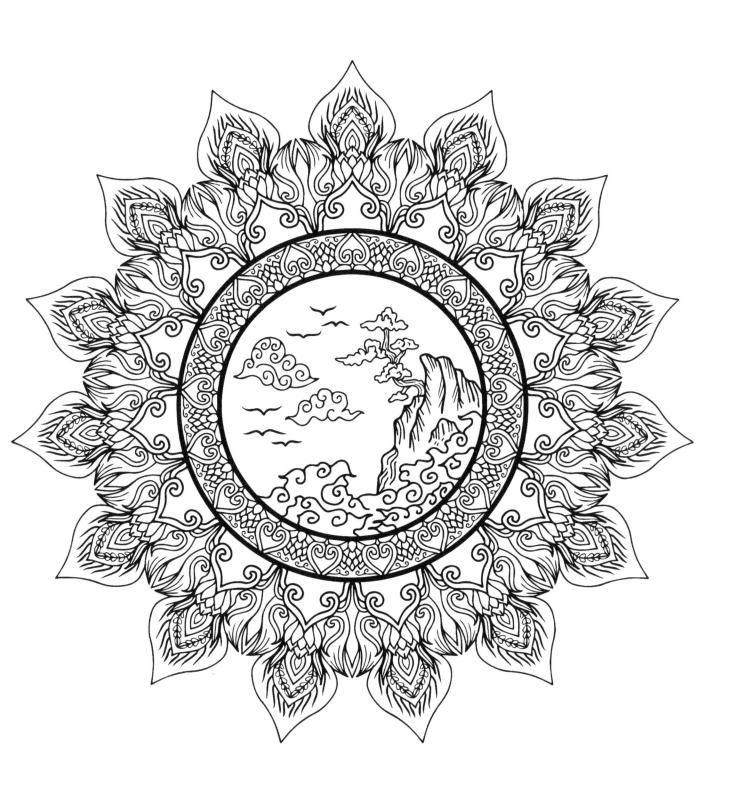

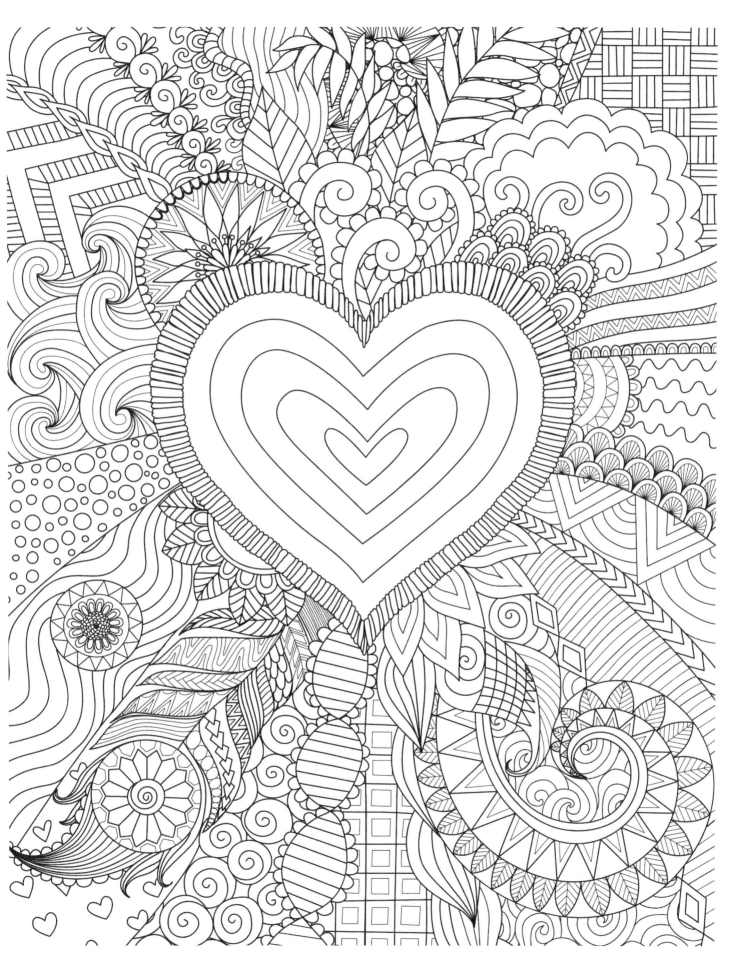

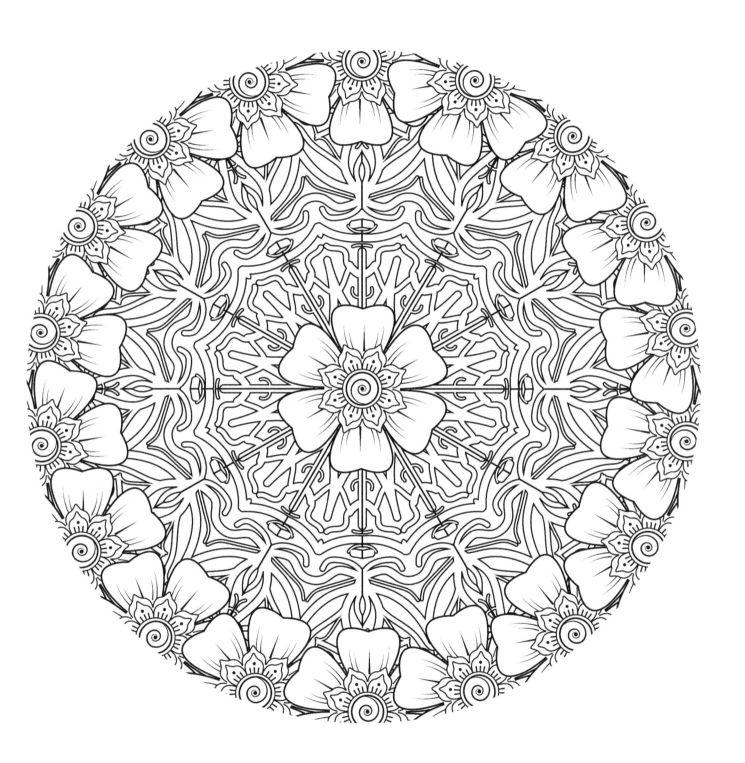

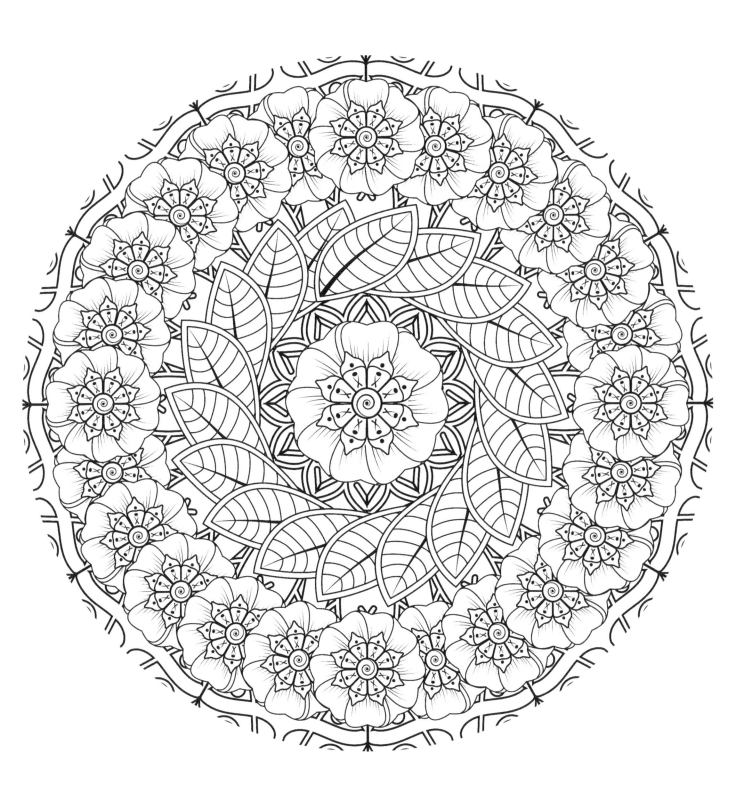

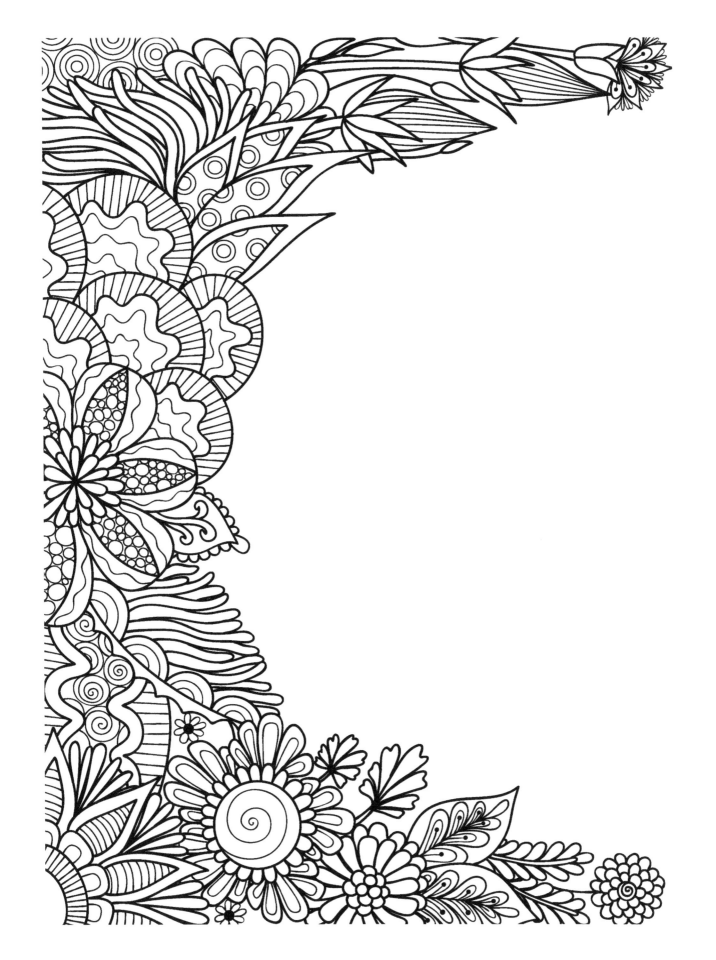

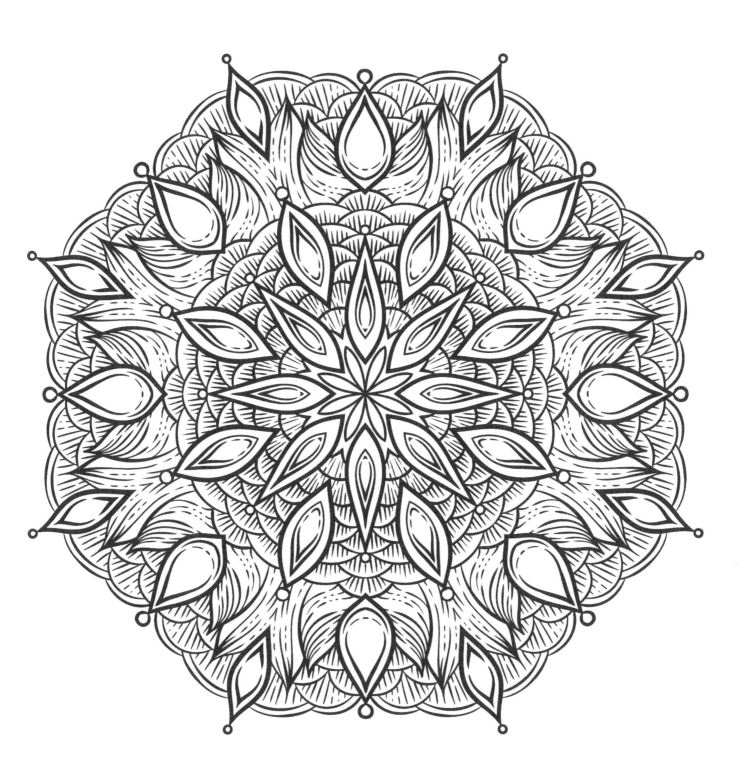

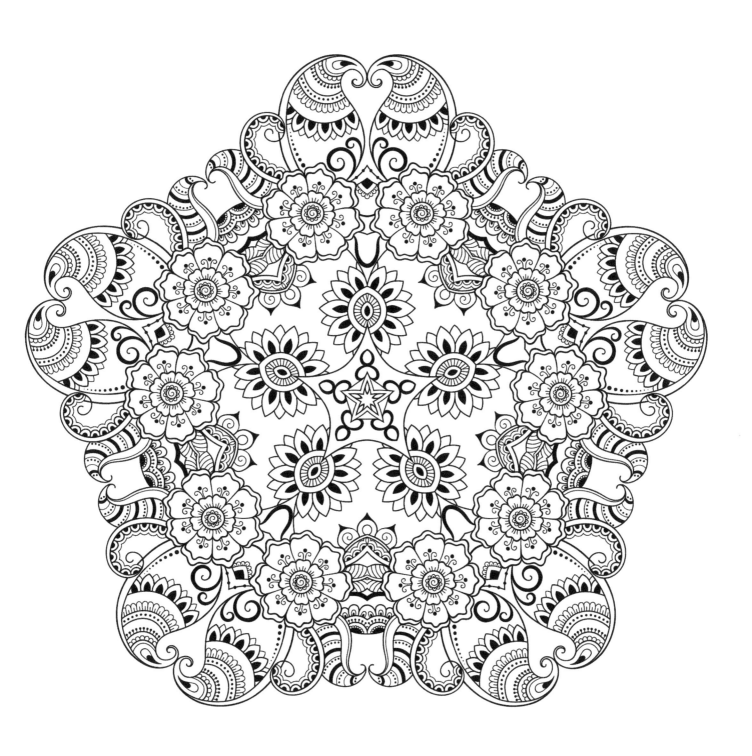

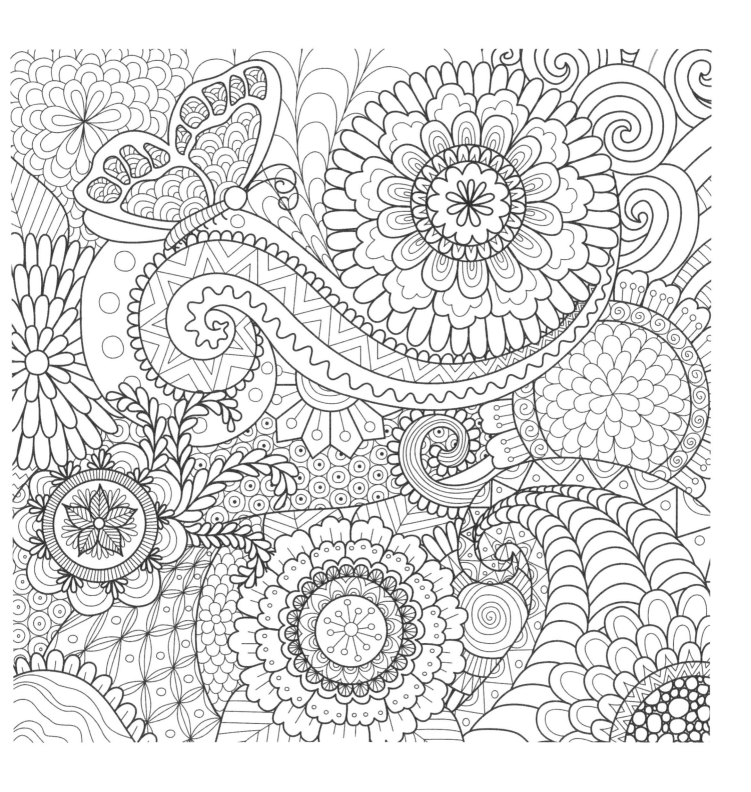

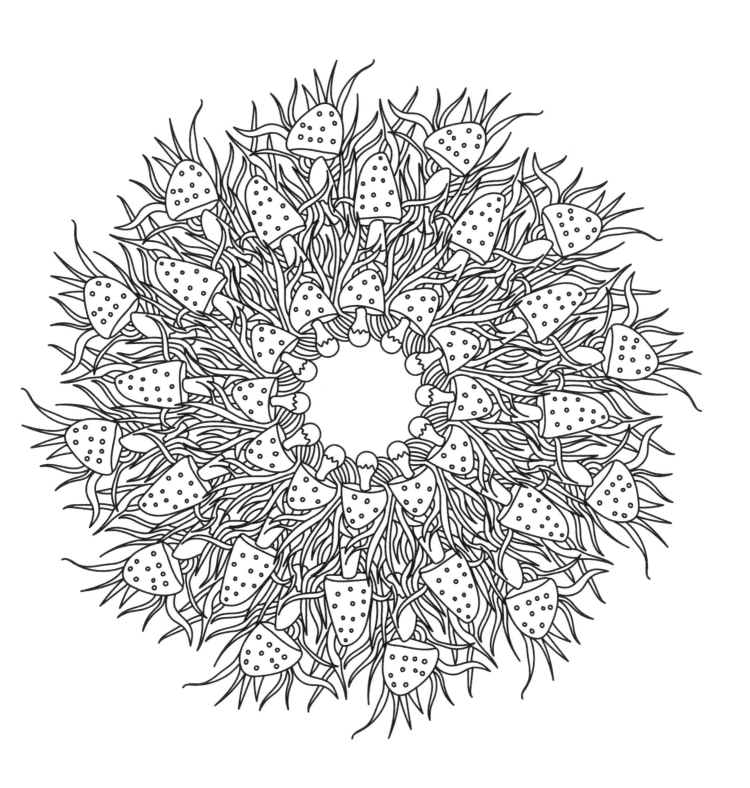

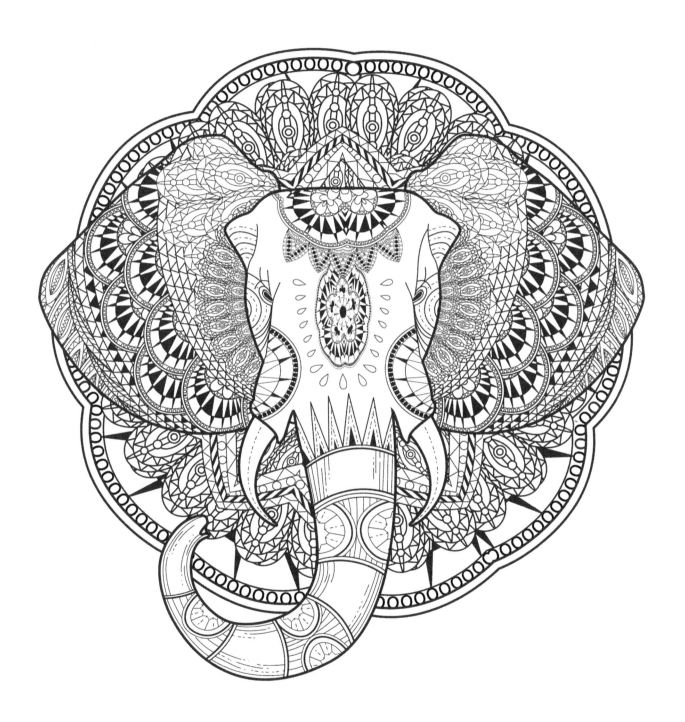

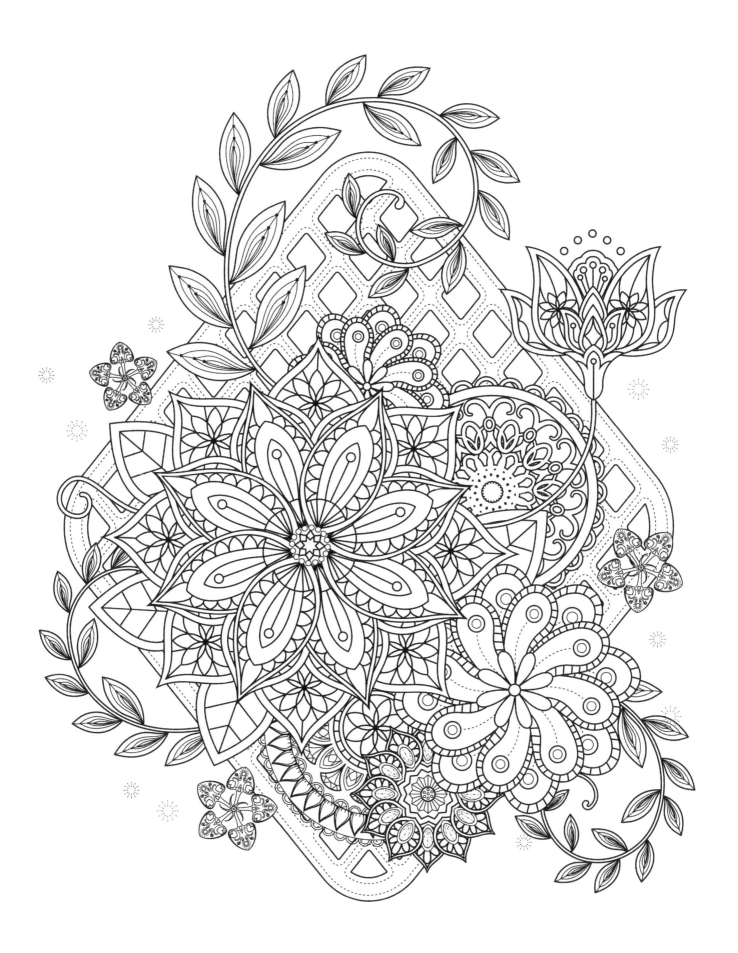

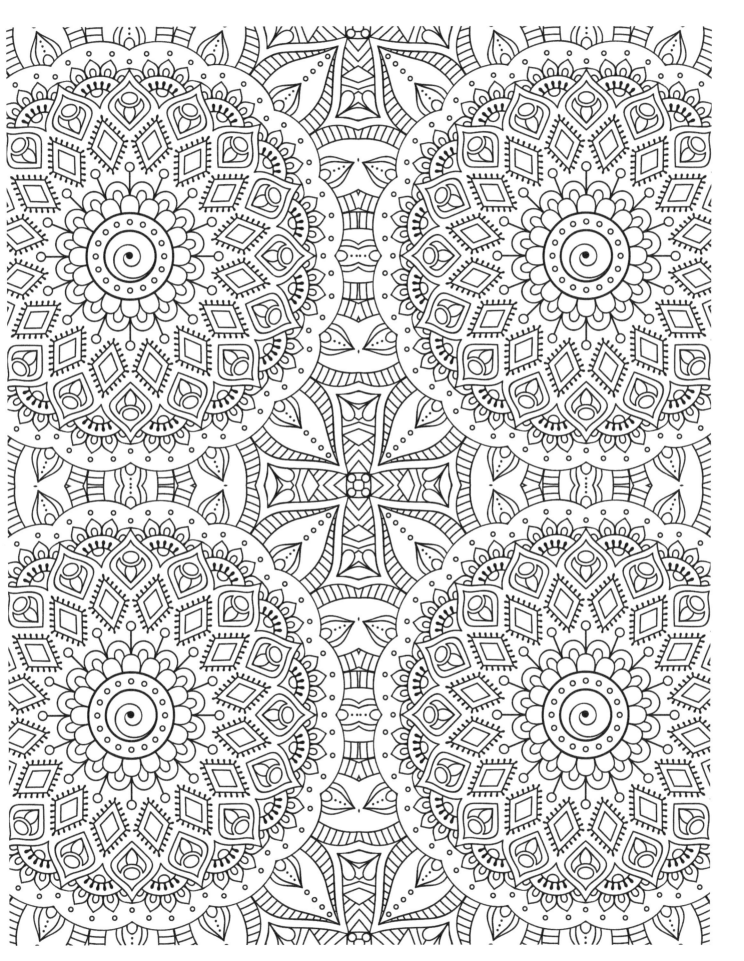

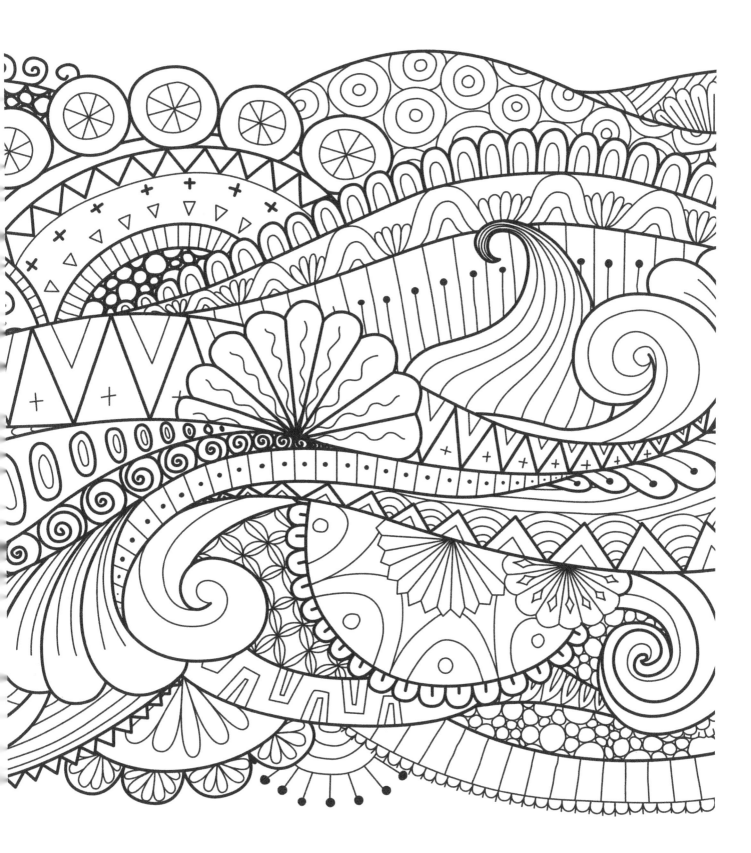

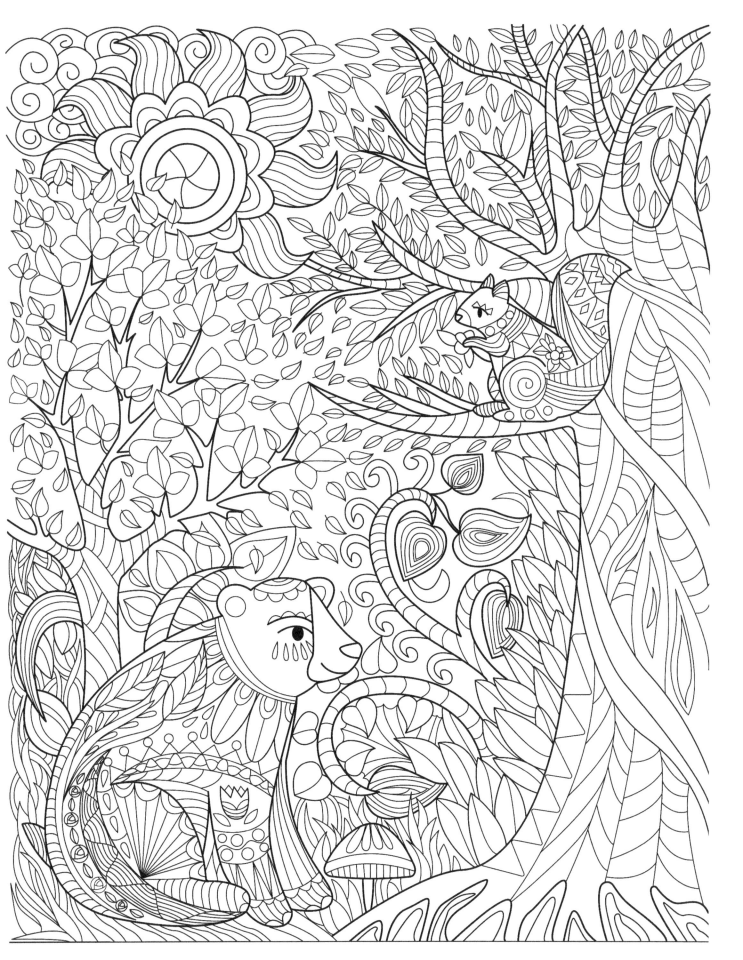

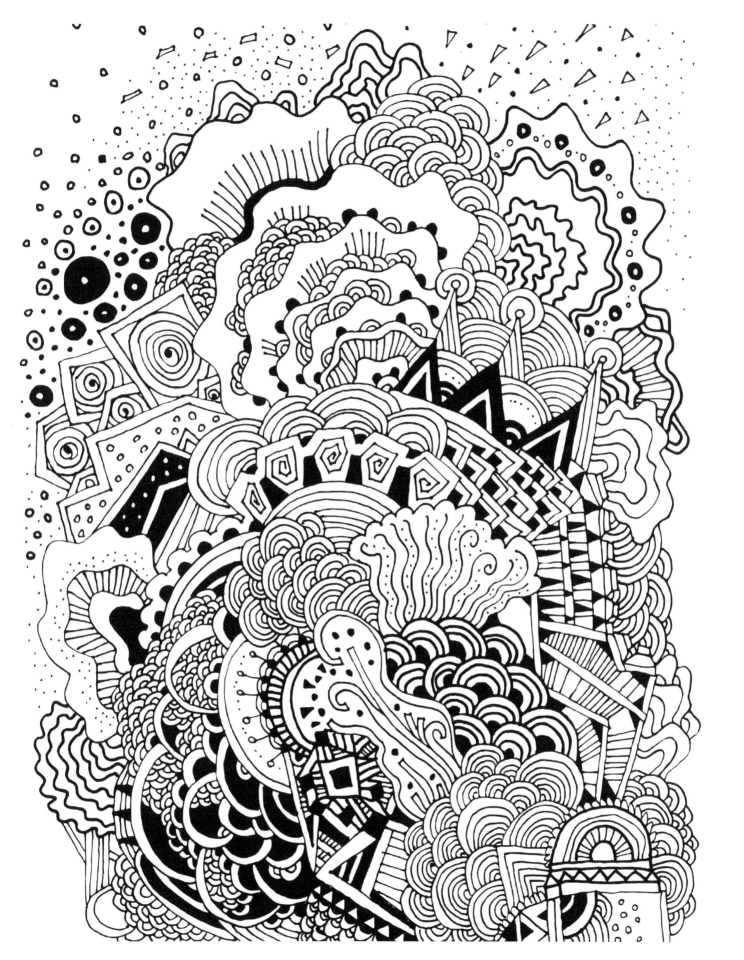

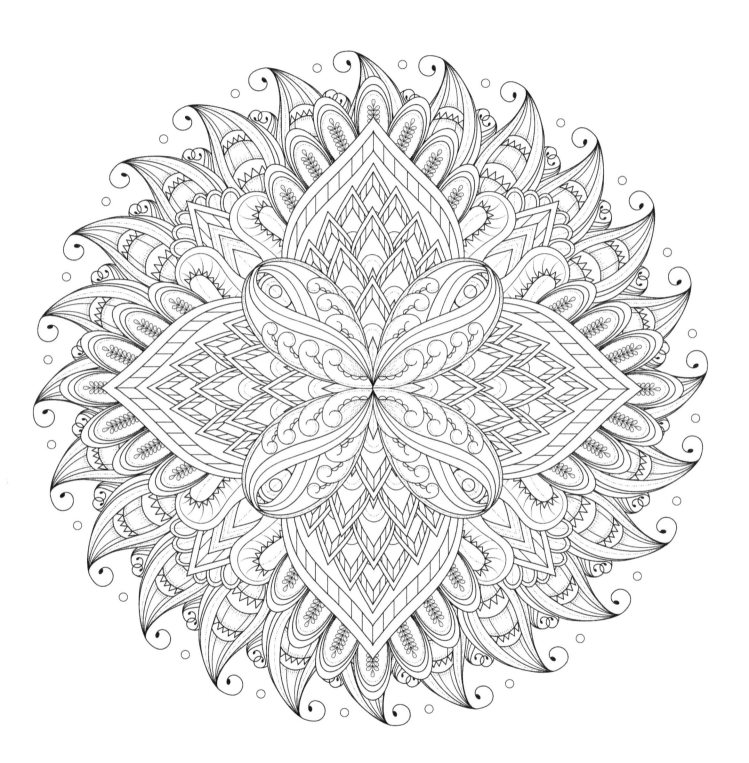

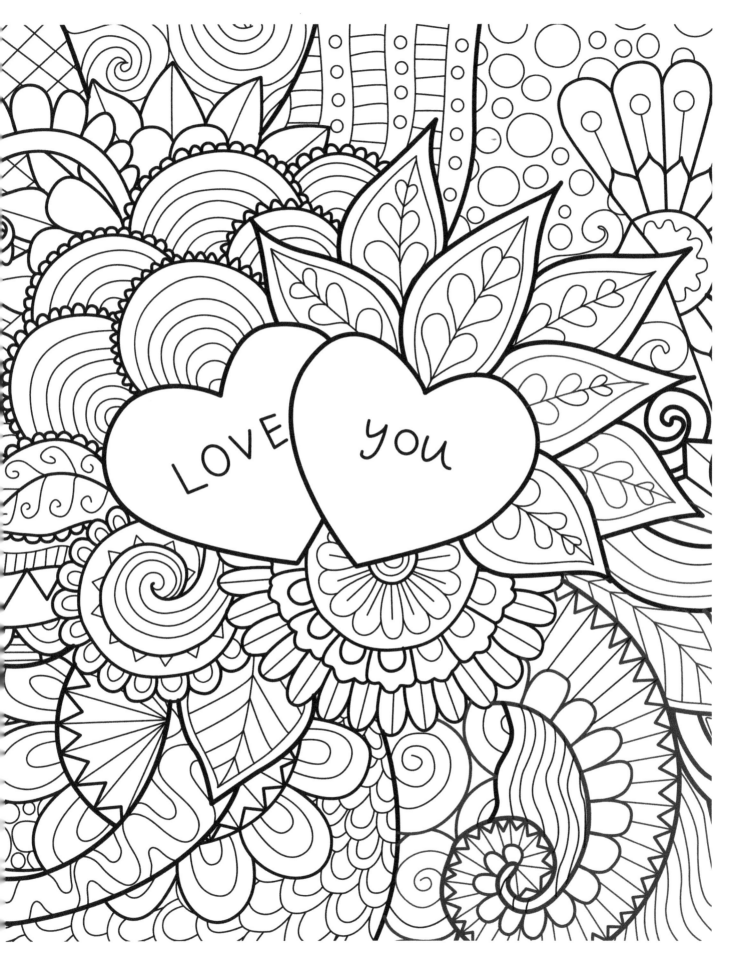

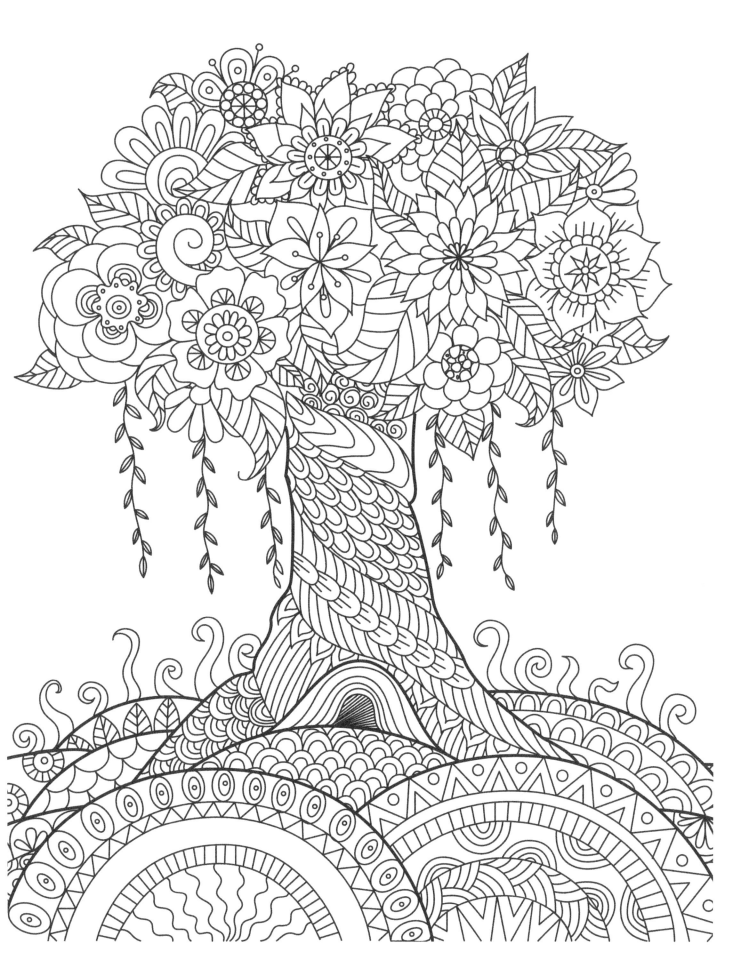

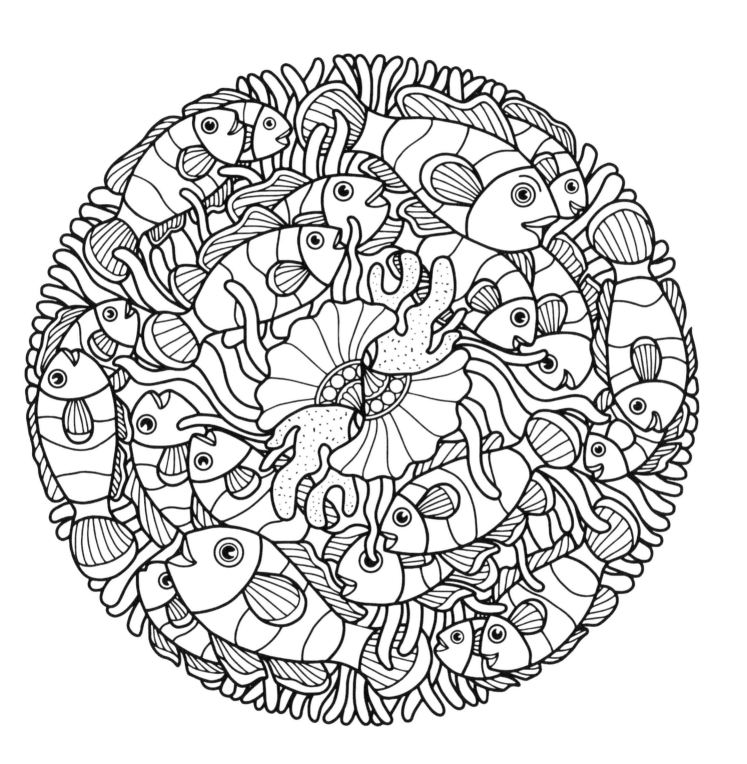

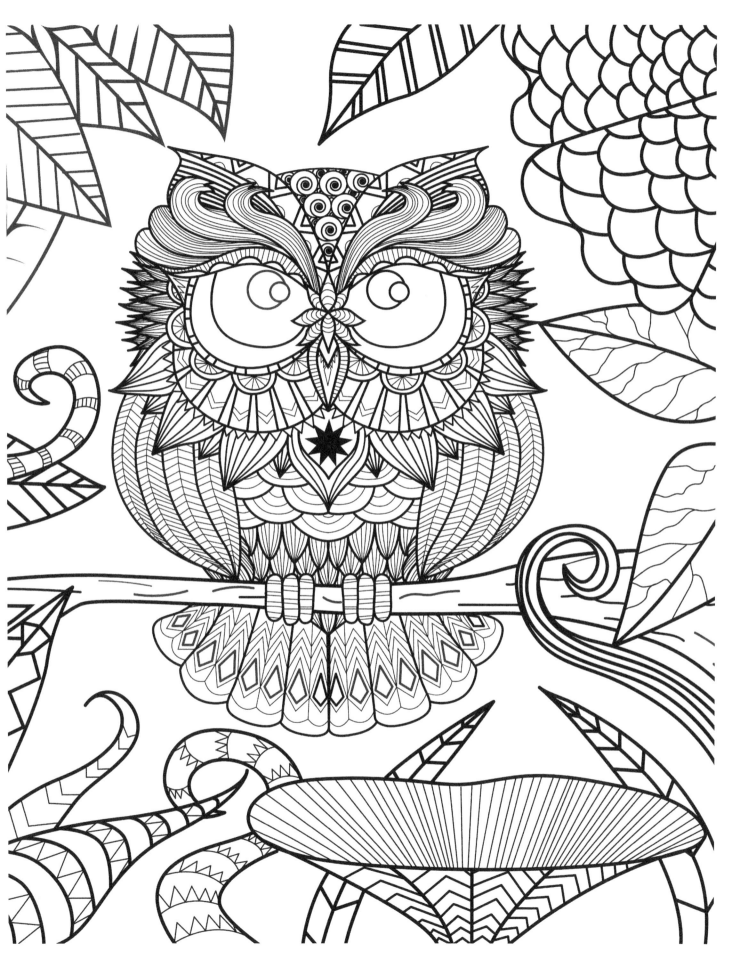

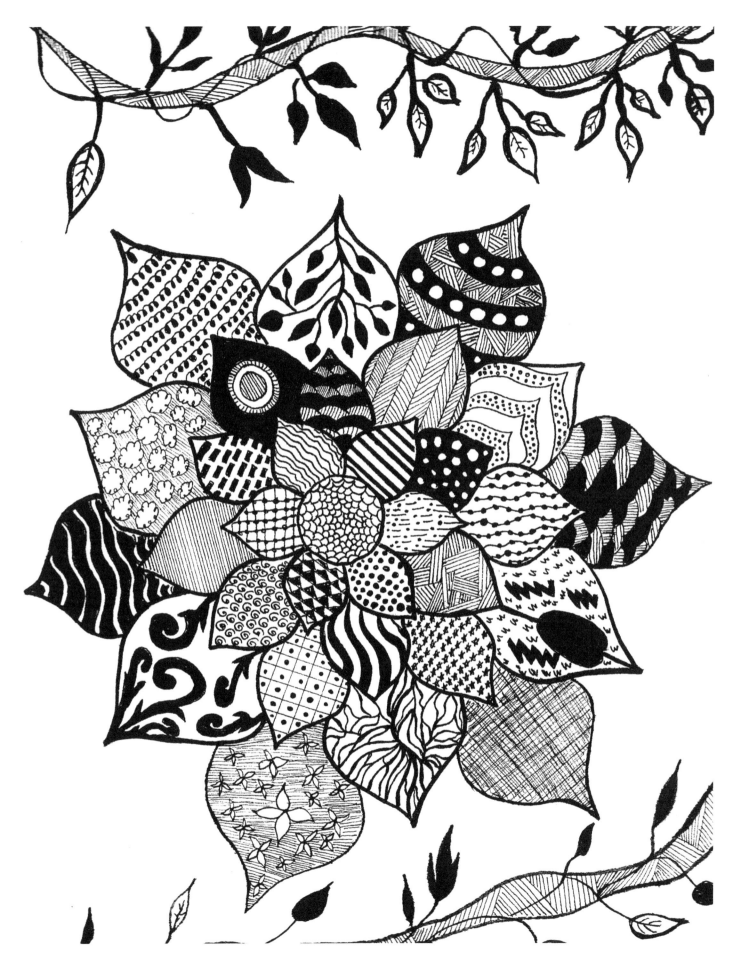

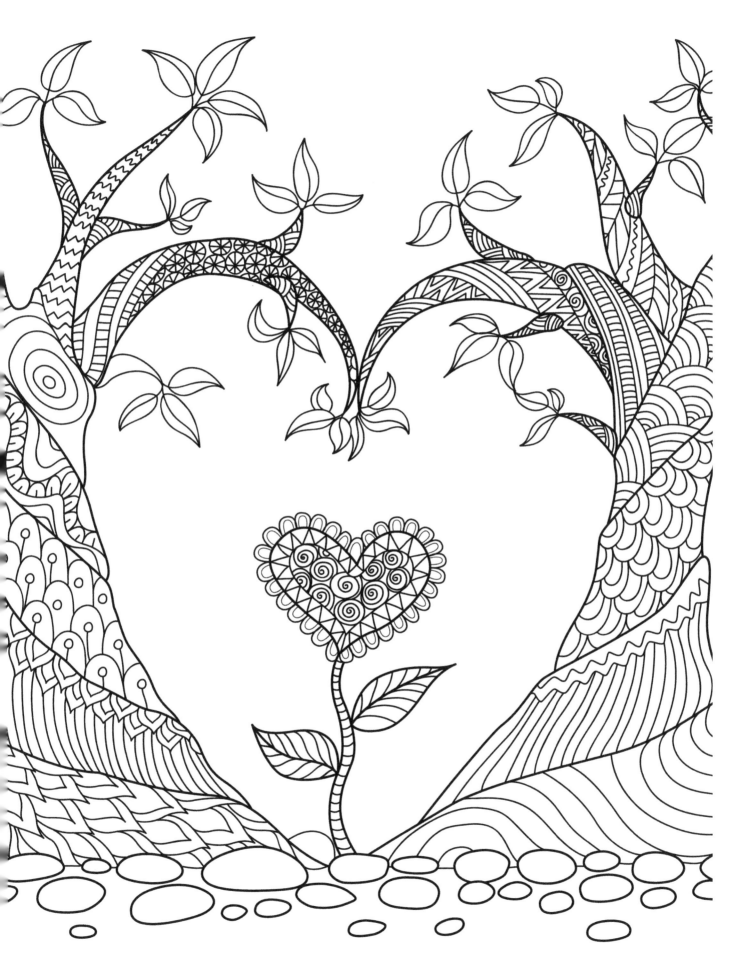

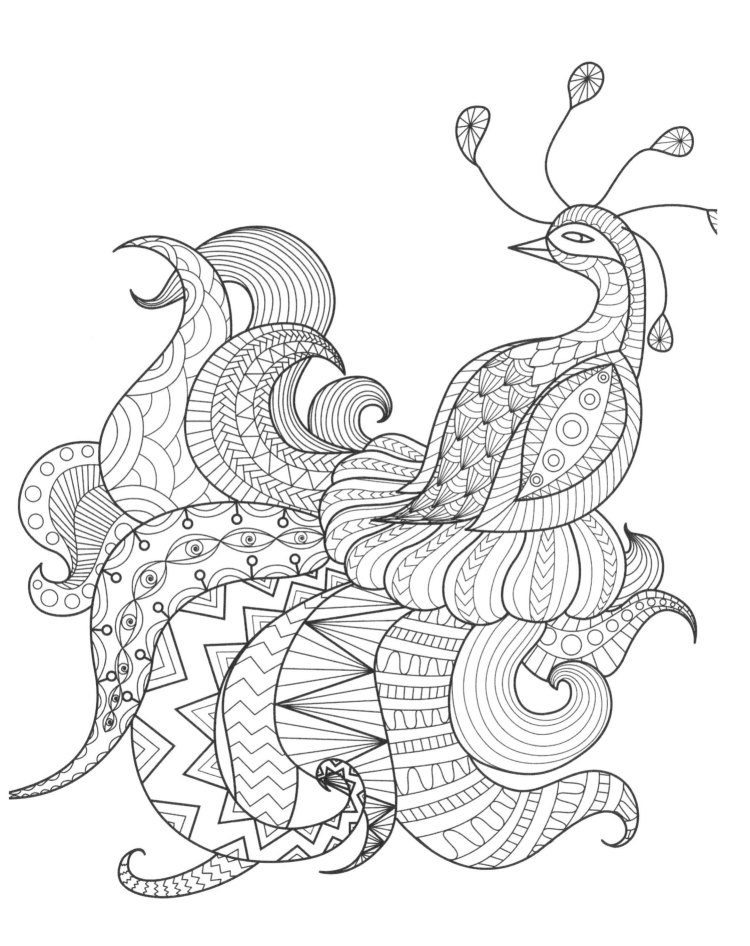

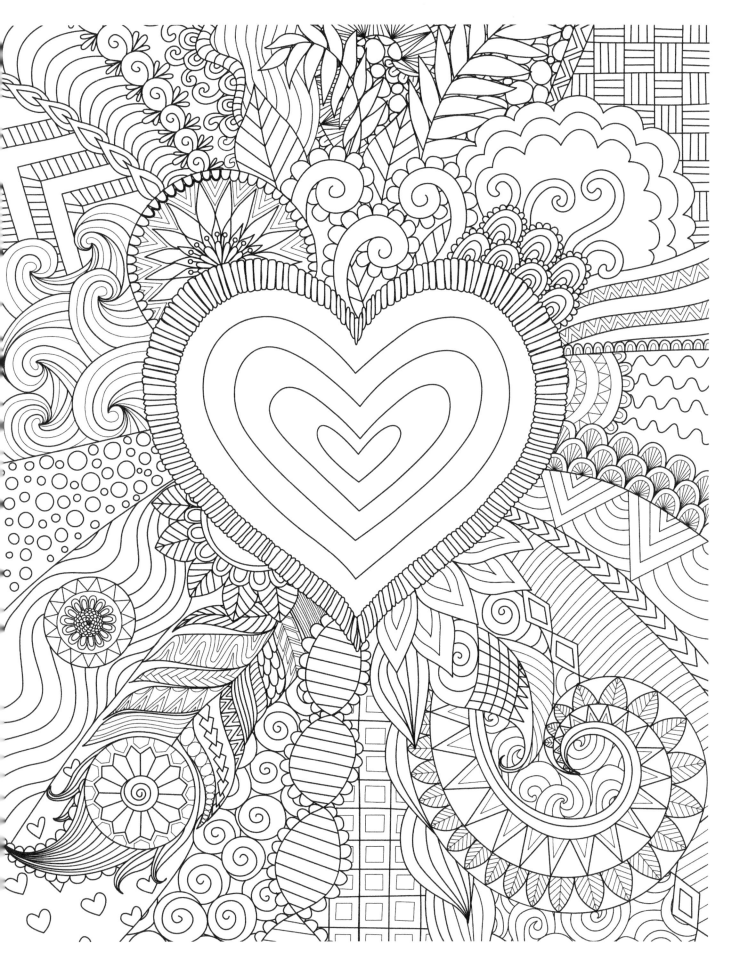

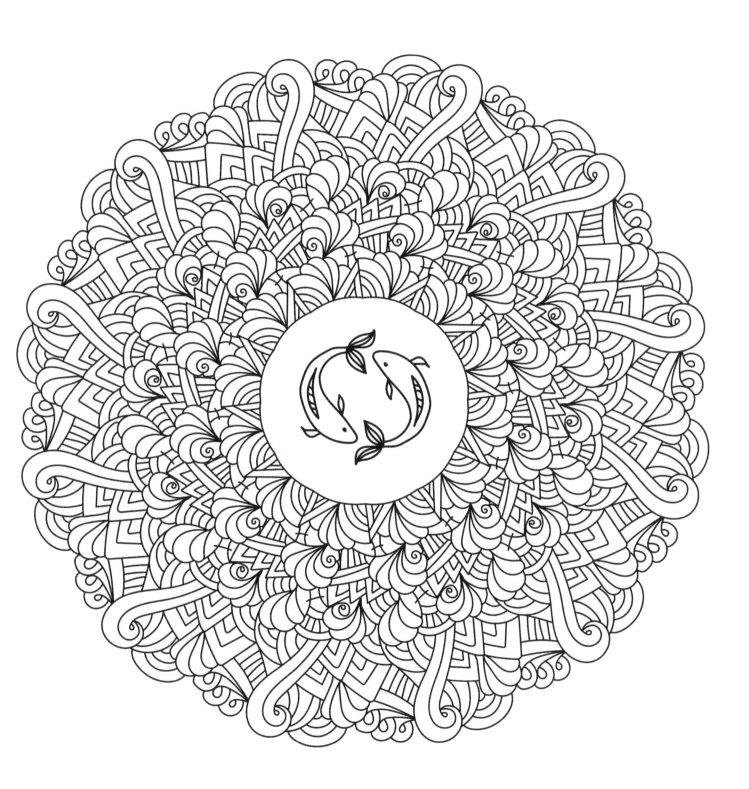

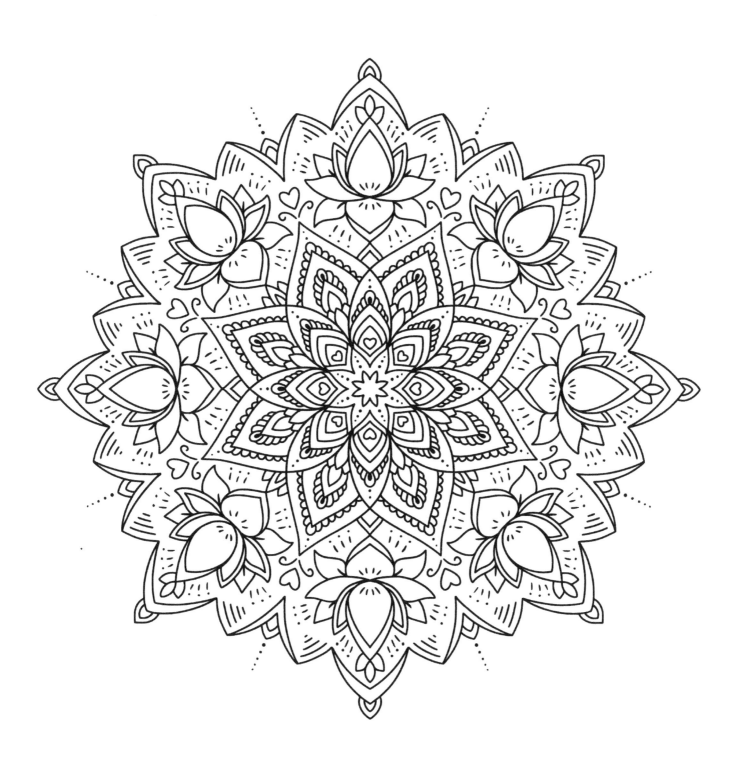

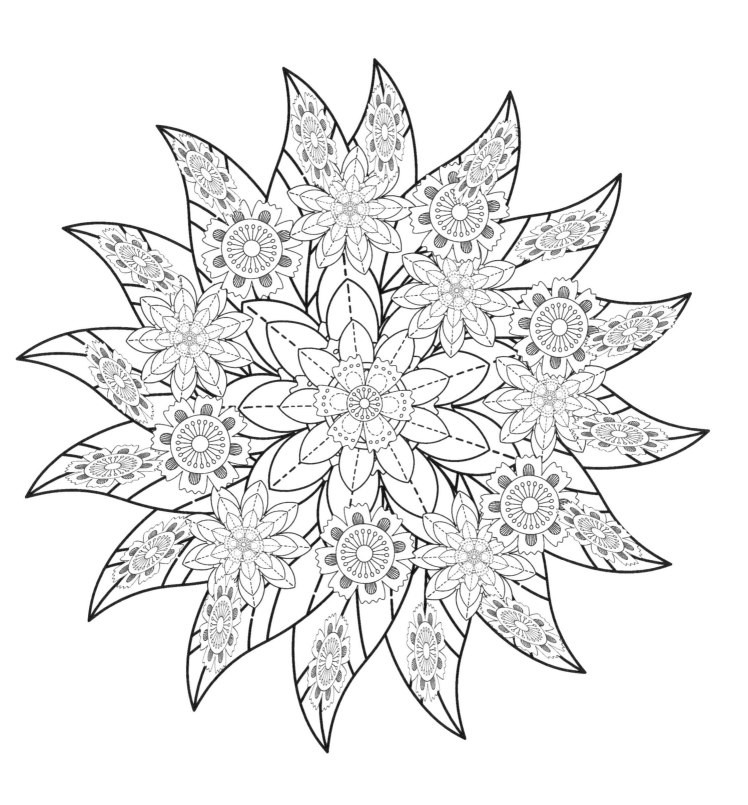

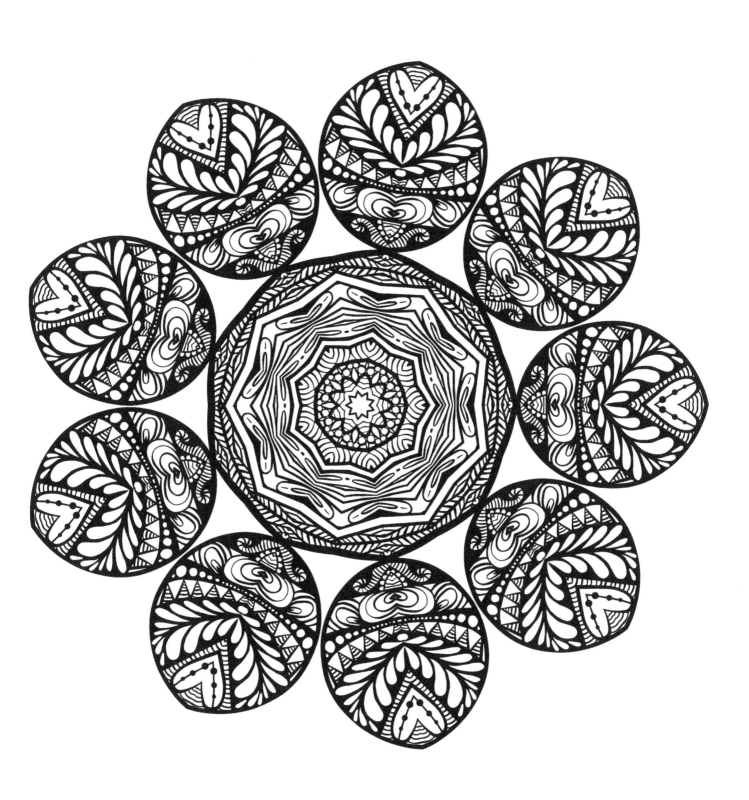

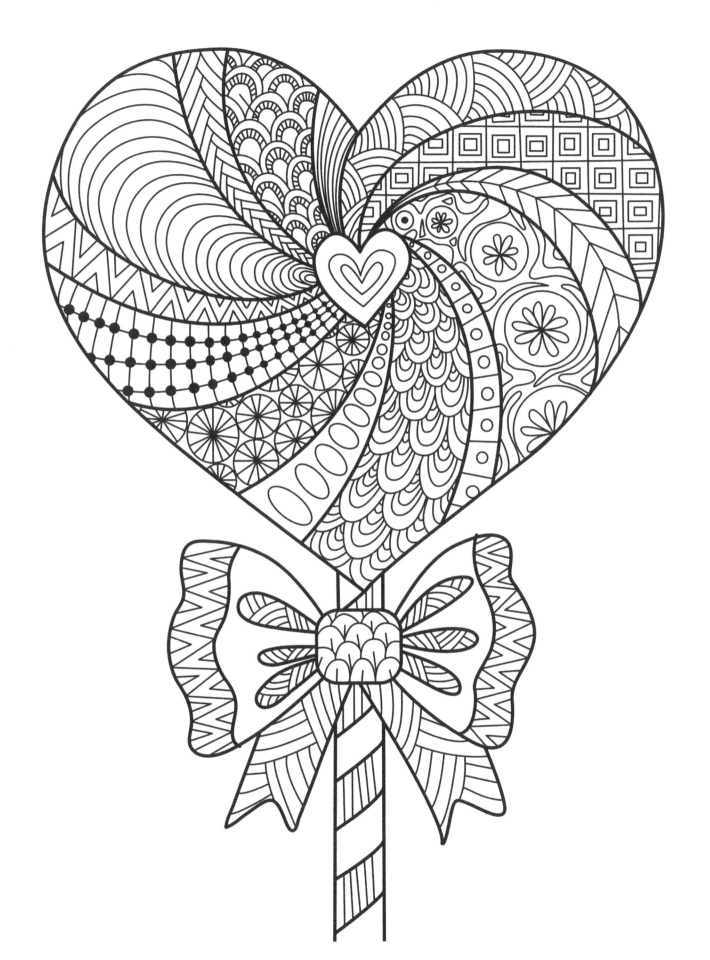

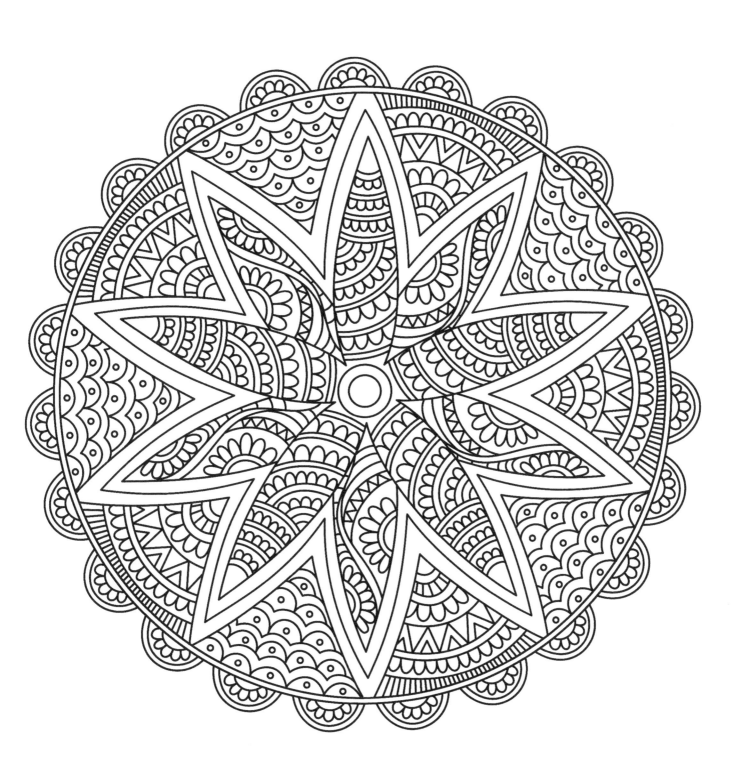

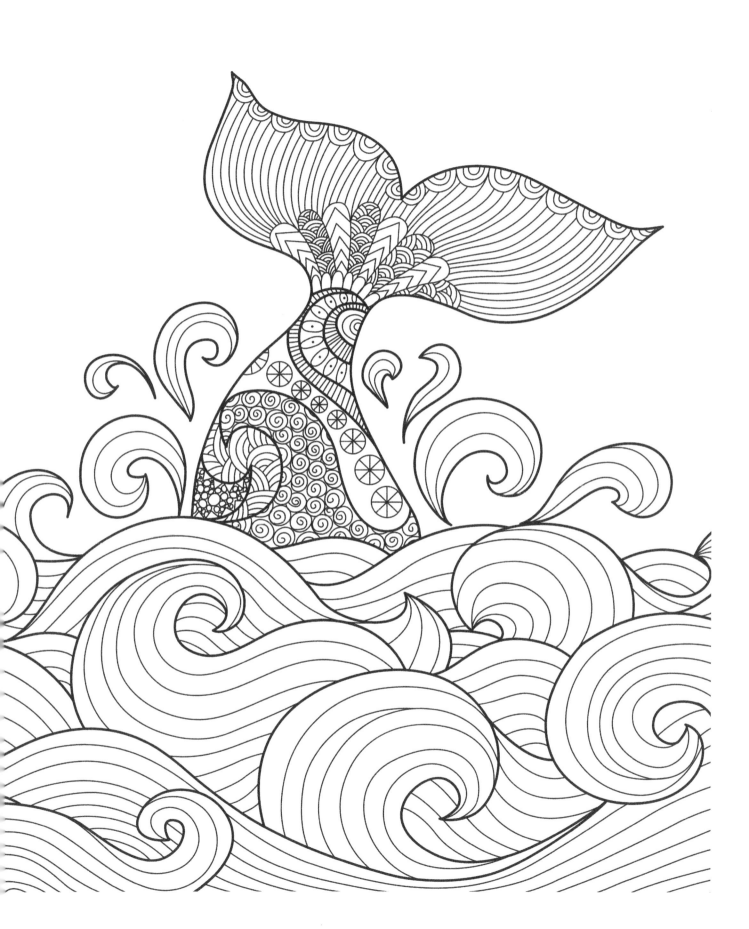

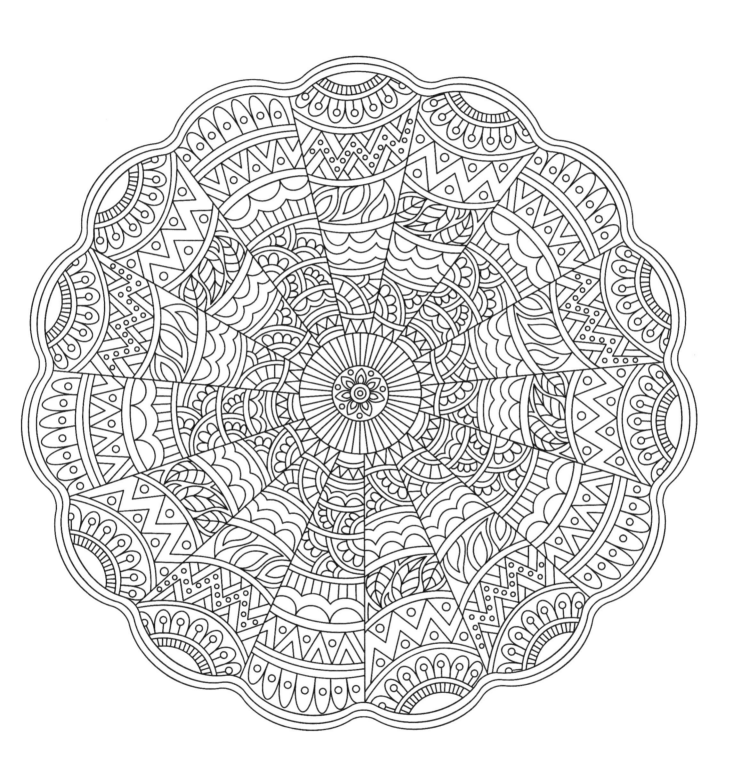

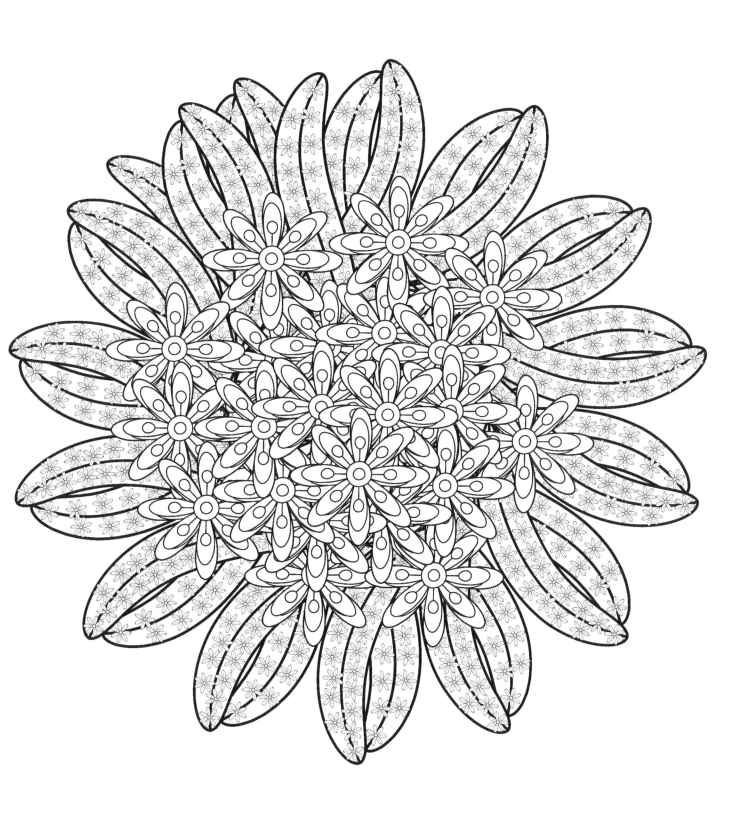

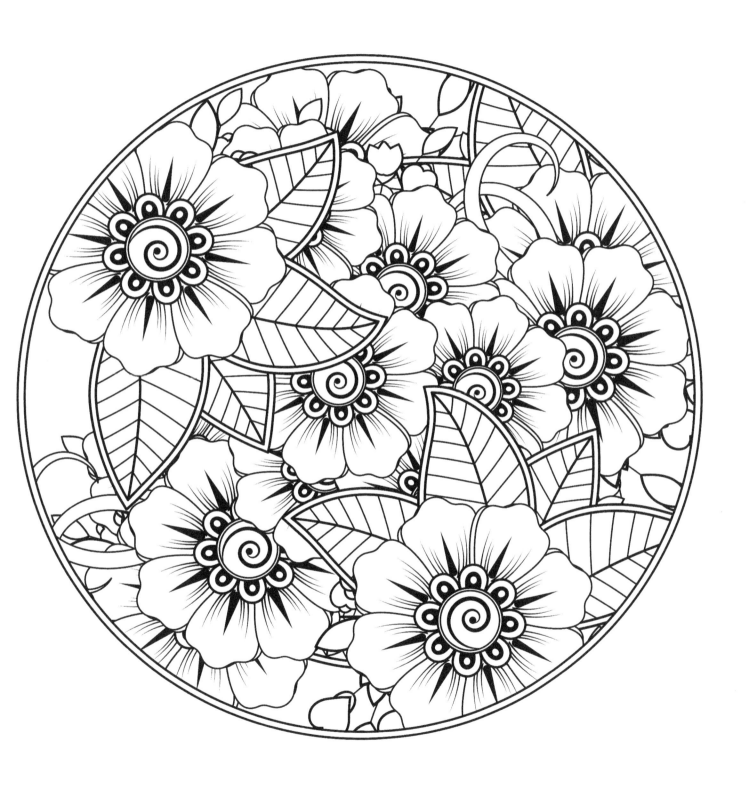

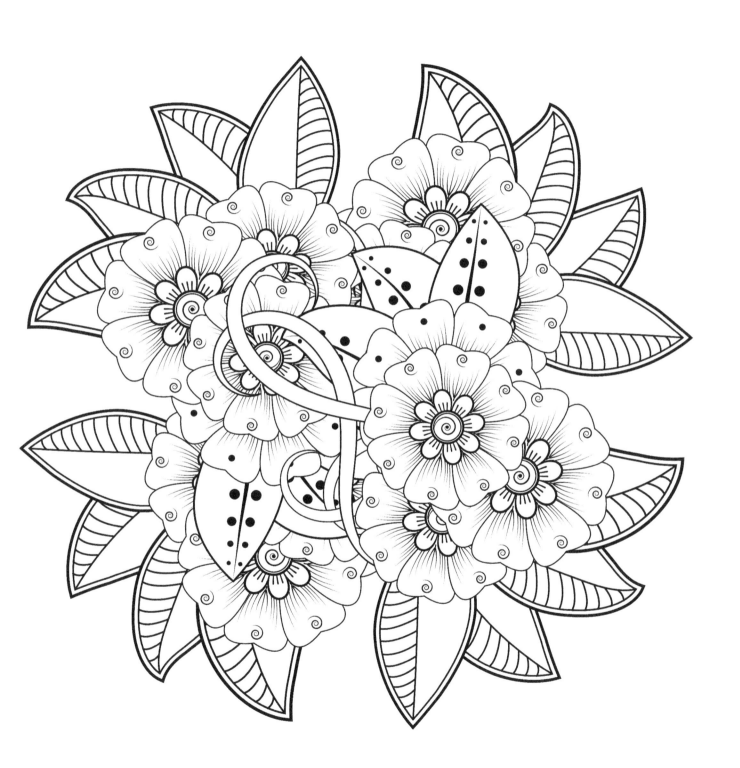

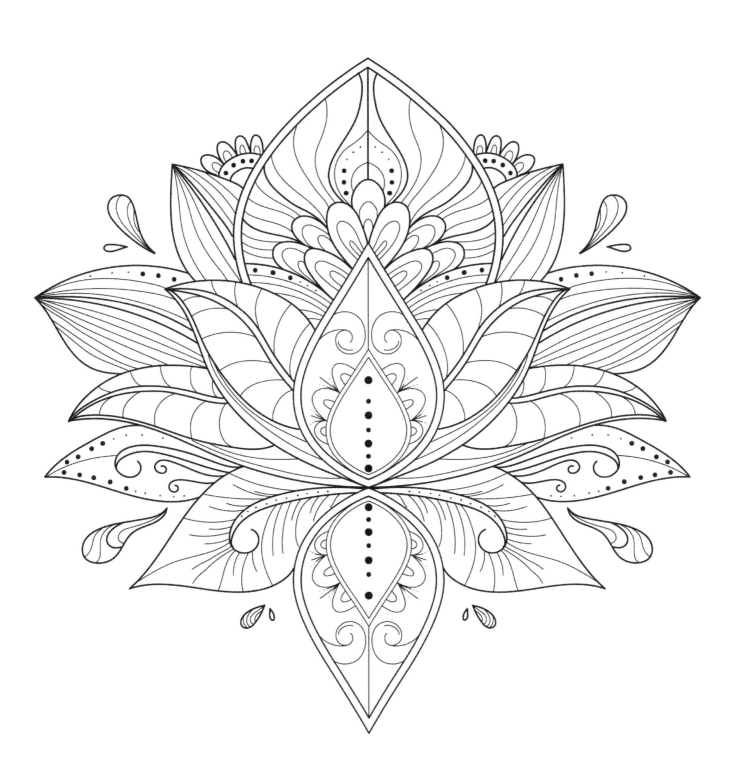

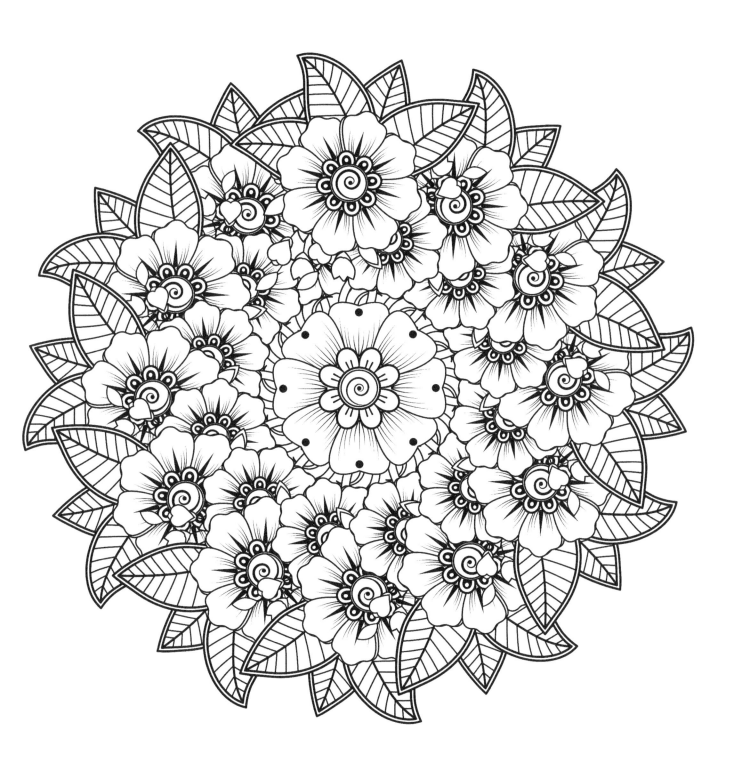

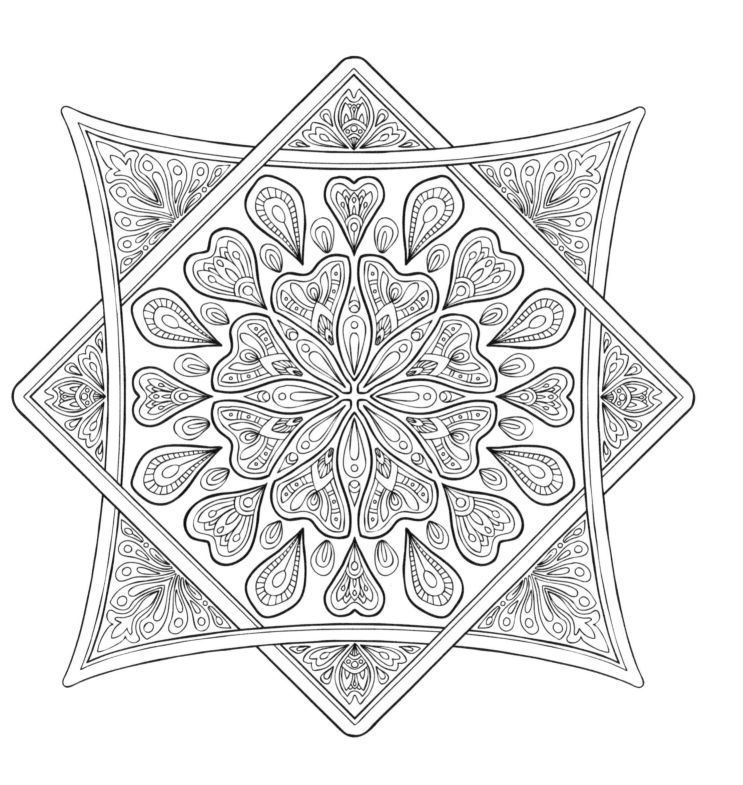

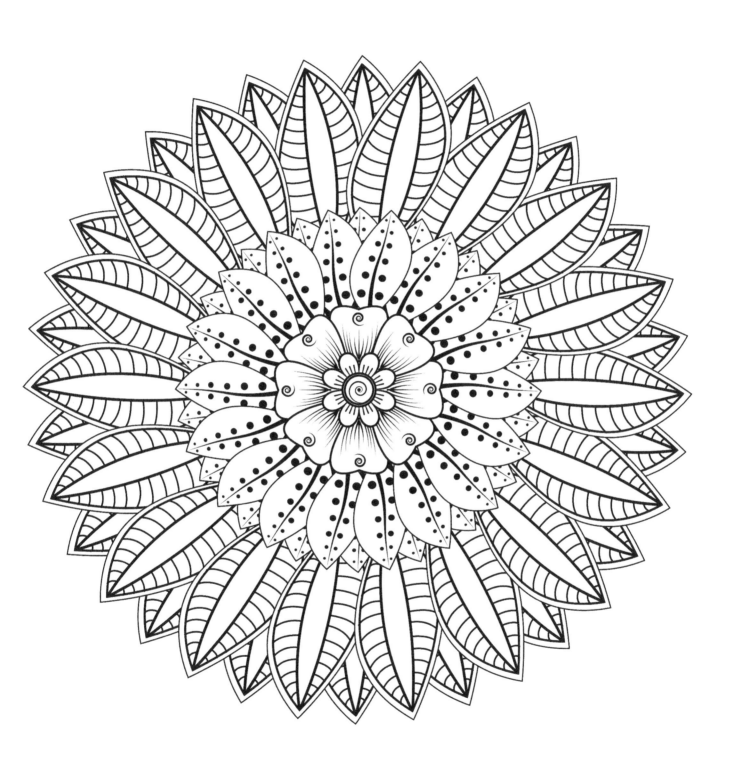

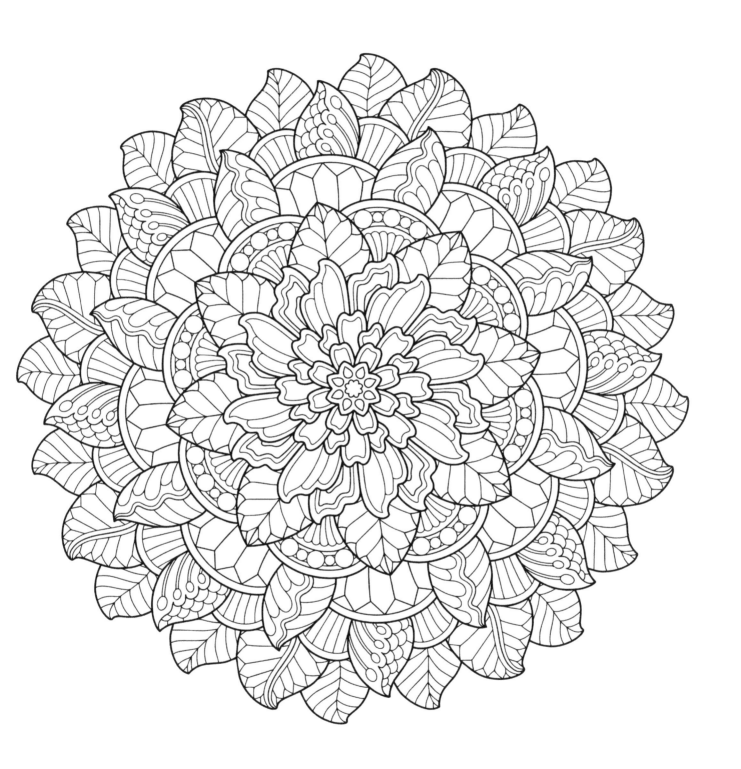

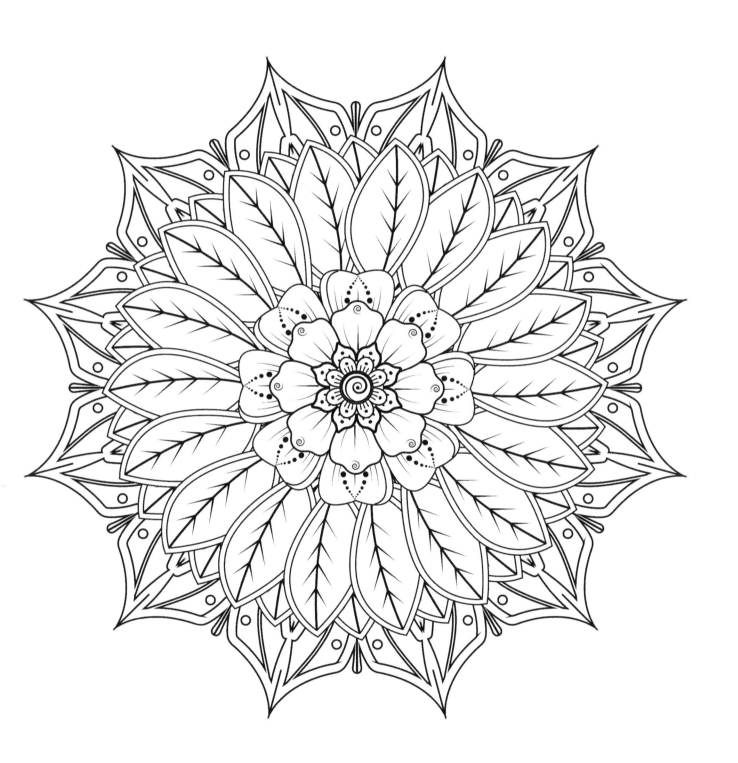

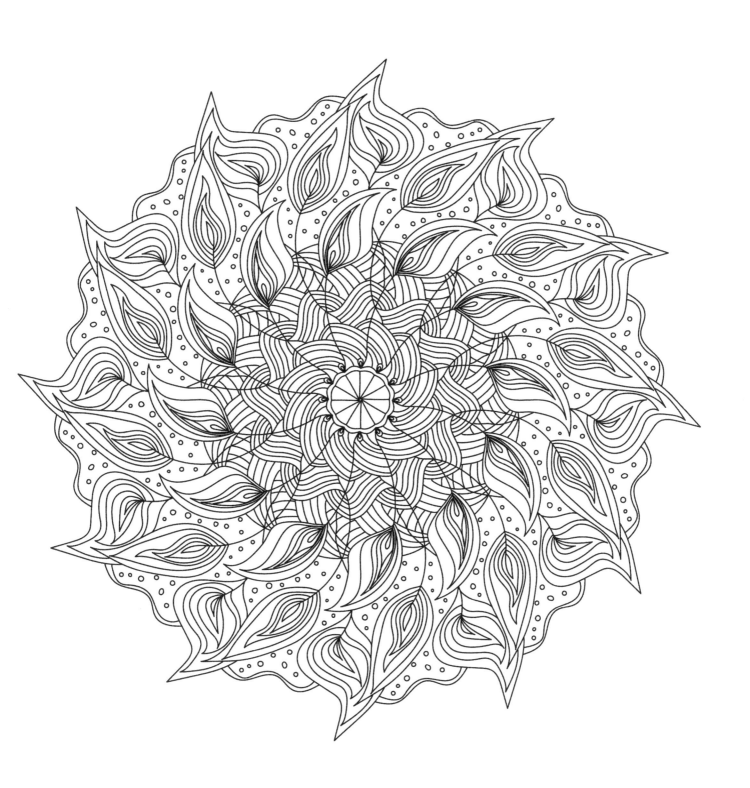

CPSIA information can be obtained
at www.ICGtesting.com
Printed in the USA
BVHW021154060623
665467BV00014B/740